@Sophie Takes a #Selfie

*Rules and Etiquette for Taking Good
Care Before You Share*

Written by
J. J. Cannon

Illustrated by
Bridget Doe

TELEMACHUS PRESS

Illustrations:
Copyright © Bridget Doe

Cover designed by Bridget Doe

Photo Credit: Lori DiVerniero of Seven Souls Studios

Published by Telemachus Press, LLC
http://www.telemachuspress.com

Visit the author website:
http://www.sophietakesaselfie.com

ISBN: 978-1-940745-44-2 (eBook)
ISBN: 978-1-940745-45-9 (Paperback)

Version 2014.02.26

Printed in the United States of America

10 9 8 7 6 5 4 3 2 1

Timeless wisdom combined with the insight and expertise of a Mom & Social Media Pro, this book is for girls ages seven to seventy-seven.

For Bryant, Sophia and Sydney

Acknowledgements

I owe a generous debt of gratitude to my wonderful family and many friends who have encouraged and supported me throughout this project.

Thank you to my sweet husband, Paul, for always sharing an honest opinion and telling me to go for it, and to my kids who have taught me the best lessons. Thank you to Bryant for your love and understanding; to Sophie, for being the inspiration for this book and for never being afraid to be yourself; to Sydney, for inspiring me to laugh more and take big chances; to Cynthia "Auntie Buttercup" Wall for your patience, wisdom, guidance, unconditional love and grammatical genius; to the Sanders family; with special acknowledgement to Brooke for making the title stand out, and to Tracy for promoting all things "Sophie" and cheering me on as a friend and fellow entrepreneur; to the entire Di Verniero family, aka the "Seven Souls", for your enthusiastic participation and encouragement. Thank you for your generosity and all that you have done to help make this little book come to life; to Bridget Doe for creating such incredible illustrations (works of art) under a tight time-frame; to my 'sister' Meg for being the best kind of friend and listener; and to my silent mentor, who shall remain anonymous, for the inspiration and your time. I appreciate all of you more than you know.

@Sophie Takes a #Selfie

*Rules and Etiquette for Taking Good
Care Before You Share*

Introduction

And The Oxford Dictionaries Word of the Year 2013 is ... *selfie!*

My name is Jennifer Cannon and I have been working professionally as a freelance writer specializing in Social Media Marketing and Management since launching JenCann Productions in 2008. After learning my way around social cyberspace, I quickly gained a reputation as a promoter of others and natural connector. I've worked with an AC Billboard Chart topping musician, a New York Times Bestselling author, and some very successful Mompreneurs.

With the evolution of all things digital and the ability to share anything and everything instantly, we're all walking a fine line between keeping it classy and uh-oh! Whether you like it or not, it's a selfie world and we're all here (and hey, they're fun!). Selfies are *everywhere*! Facebook, Instagram, ask.fm, SnapChat, spring.me, tumblr, Vimeo, Vine, Kik, WhatsApp, Whisper ... Which one is your favorite? Even as you read this, the social landscape is changing. It's enough to make anyone's head spin.

Now, despite the fact that sites like Facebook require you to be at least thirteen years of age to create an account, over 5 million users are under the age of ten according to *Social Media Today*. Most kids simply won't wait until the ripe old age of thirteen to create an account on one of the afore-mentioned sites (with or without a parent's permission). So, whether you fall into this category, or are "socially legal", let's talk about how you can put your best foot forward and think about the kind of digital footprint you want to leave behind. *Think* is the operative word here.

I write this with my own young daughters in mind as I encourage them to be the kind of girls today that the self-assured, successful women of tomorrow can look back on with confidence and pride.

I hope that reading this book will spark ongoing, open discussions in households and schools around the world. I believe it is our responsibility as parents to know what our kids under the age of eighteen are doing online. This isn't a throw-her-in-the-pool-and-see-if-she'll-swim situation. You wouldn't hand her a stick of dynamite on the way out the door in the morning and say "Have a great day sweetie! Careful you don't hurt yourself with that stick of dynamite!" A kid with a smart phone is basically walking around with most of humanity in her back pocket.

My hope is to inspire more thoughtfulness in the way young people—all people—communicate with one another. As fun and exciting as it is to be evermore connected, there is a down-side which is ultimately desensitizing and *dis*connecting us on a real and human level.

Please use this book as a tool to establish guidelines that work for your family, and keep your virtual closet skeleton-free!

Who Is Sophie?

Sophie is my daughter.

Sophie is your daughter, your sister, a friend … maybe she's your niece or granddaughter. Sophie is your teammate, your classmate, your student … she might be your neighbor. She might be you.

Sophie is not perfect. She is going to make mistakes, but together we can try to guide her in a healthy direction.

Sophie symbolizes girls of all ages, races and places.

Sophie is everyone.

The #SweetSixteen aka #Rules

Keep It Classy

Oh, snap! Before you start slinging swear words around to make a potentially un-ladylike point, go Google up a thesaurus and check out the plethora of other words (approximately a quarter of a million according to the Oxford Dictionaries) that are waiting patiently in the wings for their big break. All of this "LMFAO" and "OMFG"-ing is worn out. The poor letter 'F' is getting thrown around in acronyms all over the place. Why? Do you think it doesn't look as bad because it isn't spelled out? Well it does. And not only does it look bad, it shows a complete lack of originality.

In the heat of the moment when you're thinking about how great it's going to feel to tell that special someone to "STFU" or maybe spice up your timeline with a few expletives to make yourself appear "cool", you must understand that you cannot ever *really* take that back. Even if you change your mind and hit the delete button, it is often too late because your comment has already been seen and potentially shared, liked and/or forwarded by others. Remember, it only takes a second to capture a screenshot of *anything* online.

While we're on the subject, *please* don't swear out loud either, my loves. The absurdity of hearing a young lady channeling her inner gangsta truck driver in public is cringeworthy every time. Don't believe me? Take a moment to have a private swear-off with yourself as a Voice Memo on your phone, then listen back and have a laugh … For extra credit, go and watch the timeless brilliance of *"My Fair Lady"* starring the lady of all ladies, and my personal hero, Audrey Hepburn. Can we get #MFL trending?

Be Kind

Please refrain from using, "like"ing or sharing Hate Speak.

Knowing what to do if you see hateful or humiliating comments can be complicated. If the comments appear in your personal timeline and are directed toward you, I would advise you to delete them and block the offender immediately. Depending on the seriousness of what is being said, you may want to take a screen shot and discuss the best course of action with your parent or other trusted adult. Do not use the words "gay" and/or "retarded" along with any other racial or mean-spirited talk. The phrase "you should just go kill yourself" has become disturbingly popular and is used in various contexts.

Young people are killing themselves in record numbers over words they see printed on a screen or sent to them in text messages by cyberbullies who, thanks to technology, are almost impossible to ignore now. In a press release dated June 19, 2013 from the *CDC,* suicide is the third leading cause of death for youth between the ages of 10 and 24. Their findings show "higher suicide-related behaviors among youth involved in bullying".

Before the internet, if there was someone you were afraid of or bothered by in school, you could often find a way to avoid that person or persons. Today it is virtually impossible to escape cruel or humiliating messages that never go away. Once your words have been seen, they cannot be unseen. If you feel uncomfortable speaking up publicly there is *always* a way to speak up privately or anonymously! Go to your parent, or other trusted adult, or your guidance counselor at school. Make it clear that you want to remain anonymous, but please do speak up. Someone's life might depend on it. Know that if you choose to participate in online bullying, you should be prepared to face the potential consequences.

Take 5

Take sixty-five if you have to! Minutes that is, to calm down when you're angry. This is likely one of the most difficult rules to follow, but if you can be the master of your angry thumbs and fingers you will save yourself a lot of trouble and embarrassment. Here are a few things you can do *before* you react:

Talk to your mom, dad or other trusted adult

Talk to your dog or cat, hamster or lizard, bird, etc. (they're the best listeners)

Scream into a pillow

Sit quietly and take ten slow, deep breaths

Take a walk, like outside, without your phone (when is the last time you did that?)

Write in your journal (ironically, very private)

Call a cool headed friend (i.e., not the friend who enjoys stirring up drama)

After you have done at least one or all of these things, you will have given yourself time to do something very valuable. *Think.* Think about this. Choosing not to engage or react to a person who is directing ugliness toward you (or anyone) online says more than any of the most eloquent words or trashy acronyms you could string together. Think. Would you say this to this person's face? Would you say this to your grandmother? The moment you react without thinking to another person's insult, mean joke, etc. you immediately give them power. So, simmer down and trust me on this one.

Worry Not

The next time you catch yourself obsessing over how many people liked your picture, I want you to picture a giant, red STOP sign in front of you. Your emotional well-being and sense of self worth does not depend on how many "friends" or followers you have OR little heart "likes" under your photo. *I've seen you and you're a giant kaleidoscope of beautiful.*

Don't worry that a certain someone hasn't responded to a message that you can see has been read. Maybe she's busy … or fell and broke both of her elbows … or was in a terrible thumb wrestling accident with her brother. Maybe her phone died *just* as she was about to respond … or maybe, just maybe … your true blue friend has a busy life outside of cyberspace!

Do pay attention, without being overly sensitive, to how others treat you. You know who your real friends are, so please assume the best and stay positive.

Remember, it's not always about you!

Practice Perception

What is perception? Have you ever tried to put yourself in someone else's shoes? How do they feel? Too narrow? Are they giving you a wicked blister? Whether they're tattered and torn or shiny brand new, the important point is, they feel *different* on you.

Perception is the way that you think about something or the impression you have of it. If you can learn to shift your own perception momentarily and try to see a situation from another person's point of view, you will add an invaluable resource, not only to your social media toolbox, but to your personal character. Knowing how to do this and putting it into practice will also help you make better decisions before sharing your thoughts and pictures online. You must remember that while *you* can hear your inner voice loud and clear, and *you* know exactly the inflection and intention with which those words are being shared for all to see, no one else can.

Before you share anything, pay attention to how you're feeling at that moment and how your words and/or images will be perceived by others. Do you feel a slight tingle in your stomach? Is there a little voice in your head whispering "maybe I shouldn't"? *Listen* for that voice. It's there to help you!

For instance, if you post a snarky comment under your friend's latest selfie, followed by "jk", you might truly be "just kidding", but your readers may not be so sure.

Find Your Balance

Like anything else in life (cupcakes, tv, loud music, shopping, exercise … that boy you might have a crush on), it is important to find balance. Designate a time or times during the day and after a certain time at night (don't use your phone as an alarm clock) that you set ALL technological devices aside.

They're not going anywhere.

If you are having trouble with #WorryNot (checking your phone obsessively, having intrusive thoughts that are interfering with your ability to concentrate on schoolwork or other activities), it's time to take a break.

The 'Fear of Missing Out', or FOMO, has been an issue for kids (and adults) long before anyone had the ability to share everything-that-is-more-fun-and-fabulous-about-their-lives-than-yours. In reality, we have all become our own public relations spin doctors—don't believe the hype, you're not ever *really* missing out on much.

If you are feeling anxious, overwhelmed or out of control, please talk to your parents, school counselor or other trusted adult as soon as possible. Just because social media is available to everyone does not mean that it's healthy for everyone.

Be Queen Bee

Who wouldn't love being Queen? I hereby pronounce you Royal Queen of your digital kingdom! Go forth and declare zero tolerance for your castle walls being sullied up with atrociousness of any kind. You control who has access to any of your social accounts, which is why I highly recommend keeping them as private as possible at all times ... like a virtual moat.

Now that you're wearing the crown, how will you wield your power?

Is it "popular" to be mean?

Historically speaking, mean girls usually wind up lonely and miserable. Not the most popular? Good! Be the sole leader of *you*. Be original. Beware of becoming such a big fan of others that you forget about your own biggest fan ... YOU!

Following the crowd is the exact opposite of original. No matter your social status, be a positive role model, surround yourself with positive people, and cultivate Royal Girl Power!

Keep It Real

In the mystical Land of Social, whether we're talking about kid land or grown-up land (often eerily similar), perception is reality. In other words, if I am not a close personal friend of yours, I will make my own assumptions about you based on what you share.

Generally speaking, we tend to portray the best of what's going on in our lives and about ourselves. *There is nothing wrong with this.* It is important to keep in mind, however, that people you might come into contact with online that you don't know personally (i.e., anyone other than classmates, actual-real-life friends, family members) can pretend to be anything or anyone they want to be.

If you are in your teens, you may be learning about branding yourself, so the general message here is avoid trying to be someone you are not in order to please or impress others. This will only make you unhappy.

Authenticity breeds happiness.

Establish Respectful Boundaries

The way you behave and present yourself online (and in the real world) teaches others how to treat you. Make the decision now that you will keep healthy boundaries for yourself and expect the same from anyone you come into contact with online. As an example, if someone uses disrespectful language or makes embarrassing comments on your posts, in your 'feed' or on your timeline, that person should be warned and/or blocked immediately. By doing this you are sending a clear message to let people know exactly where you stand.

And now, a little story.

Once upon a time, in sixth grade, there was a neighborhood kid, we'll call him Dan, who used to refer to me as "Hey, Bozo" every morning on our walk to the bus stop. Of course, I had a mad crush on him. There were four of us who walked together, including another kid, John, who is still a dear friend today. John and Dan were good friends, but one day, to my surprise, John told Dan to knock it off. John had asked me recently why I let Dan call me Bozo and generally embarrass me. I don't remember my answer, but I'll never forget the lesson I learned from that situation. Because I did not possess much self-esteem at the time, I went along looking all googly-eyed at Dan, completely oblivious to the fact that he was a total jerk. I lacked my own sense of self-respect and he knew he could walk all over me.

Don't be afraid to let people know who you are and where *you* stand right from the beginning!

Tuesday at 6:08 PM

Tuesday at 6:09 PM

Tuesday at 6:10 PM

Check Yourself

If you are updating your status or, according to the *Urban Dictionary*, "changing your profile pic more than you're changing your clothes", it's time to dial it back a notch … or three.

Unless you're a food blogger, we don't need to know what you ate for breakfast, lunch and dinner today. It is also unnecessary to report publicly how much you just spent on clothes or shoes or anything, or how much you really, really love your best friend who is perfect (which is really kind of an insult to your other friends). No one wants or needs a running commentary of your entire day— which, by the way, takes up a lot of valuable time. Allow me to break it to you gently. No one, not even the most famous of celebrities, is that interesting.

Now, about the selfies … I get it! Who doesn't love a fun selfie? It isn't necessarily a negative thing. My nephew (a college student) recently pointed out that taking selfies are the only moments in which we have complete control over our own images.

Selfies can be empowering and beautiful.

On the flip side, the digital age has made us all a bit more narcissistic and self-aware. Don't get so caught up in capturing moments that you actually miss the moment.

Rest Your Thumbs, Flap Your Gums

Put your phones and tablets away! When is the last time you looked someone in the eyes and really listened? Whether you have realized it yet or not, you are losing the ability to have a real life conversation.

Our devices have become vices. Take a break.

The minute you are bored or potentially uncomfortable, what do many of you do? You reach for and hold on tightly to your phones (which are probably already in hand) and stare intently into the cyber abyss. Am I right? Yes.

Frequently checking your phone while you're out with friends is rude—period. Audrey Hepburn would totally agree. Put them away. Just do.

Does your school allow cell phones in the lunch room? If so, I challenge you to put all cell phones in the center of the table and see who lasts the longest. If you succeed and no one touches their phones for the entire lunch period, congratulations! How did it feel? You can tell me about it by first getting permission to post a picture to Instagram or Twitter. Then tag @sophieselfie and use hashtag #sophieselfiechallenge.

Having a party? Decorate a cute basket and ask everyone to deposit their phones as they enter. Then pay attention to how much fun you have without them! I spoke with a mom and her teenage daughter who told me they did this recently at an annual party. They both agreed it was the best party ever.

Exercise Empathy

em·pa·thy *noun*—the ability to understand and share the feelings of another.

Think before you comment. Take a few extra moments to consider how what you are about to say might affect another person. Think before you "Like" or share another person's comment or photo. Consider how you might feel if the situation were reversed.

It shouldn't surprise anyone that most kids under the age of twelve have very little impulse control or filter. Examples of this are not hard to find. A friend posts a pic of her new nail polish and kids being, well, *kids*, sometimes find humor in making a rude comment (e.g., "Ugly!"). The kid who made the comment probably didn't think much about it and clearly had no concept of what kind of effect it might have.

> New research published in Developmental Psychology ... reports that cognitive empathy, the mental ability to take others' perspective, begins rising steadily in girls at age 13. However, boys don't begin to show gains in perspective-taking until age 15, which helps in problem-solving and avoiding conflict.
> —The Wall Street Journal Online, *Teens Are Still Developing Empathy Skills*

Children under the age of nine have not yet fully developed the cognitive skills to truly understand the concept of empathy. Why am I sharing this fact with you? Because I've seen seven and eight year olds with Facebook accounts ... which have not been made private.

Every child develops differently which is why I encourage every parent to seriously consider waiting to allow children under the age of thirteen to become active on any social platform.

Beware the Over-Share

Check yourself before you wreck yourself, please! Keep in mind that everything you share starting from <u>enter your grade here</u> until you head off to college is going to follow you.

Gone is the feeling of relief one once possessed after leaving behind, let's say, an embarrassing high school experience or those awfully awkward middle school days. Today, prospective college roommates or bosses are going to Google you first and ask questions later.

Adding your new college friends or co-workers on facebook? Now they can look back at who you "used to be". What will they see? How many potentially embarrassing photos are there of you floating around that a bitter ex-boyfriend or frienemy might choose to unearth at the most inopportune moment?

Proceed With Caution

In the name of respect for yourself and others, please refrain from sharing inappropriate materials or photos of yourself or anyone else! Before you start snapping pics of you and your besties anywhere at any time, STOP! Then ask yourself these three things first:

1. Do I have permission from my friends (or acquaintances) to take the picture?

2. Will anyone be potentially embarrassed, hurt or offended?

3. Will anyone (including me) be mortified if someone were to capture a screenshot and share it with the world (or my mother)?

And guess what? Those SnapChat pics? Turns out they may not ever *really* disappear.

Can we please stop with the fish-lipped kissy faces already—can you say "premature wrinkles", darlings? Please stop trying to grow up so bloody fast—you've got your whole lives ahead of you to be sexy, doe-eyed minxes … in PRIVATE! Also, If you insist on taking photos of yourselves in bathrooms wearing outfits that you definitely were not wearing when you left your house, showing more skin than a hairless cat, please at least crop out the toilet. Or, how about just be a lady? That is all. #MFL (finally, an "F" we can get behind!)

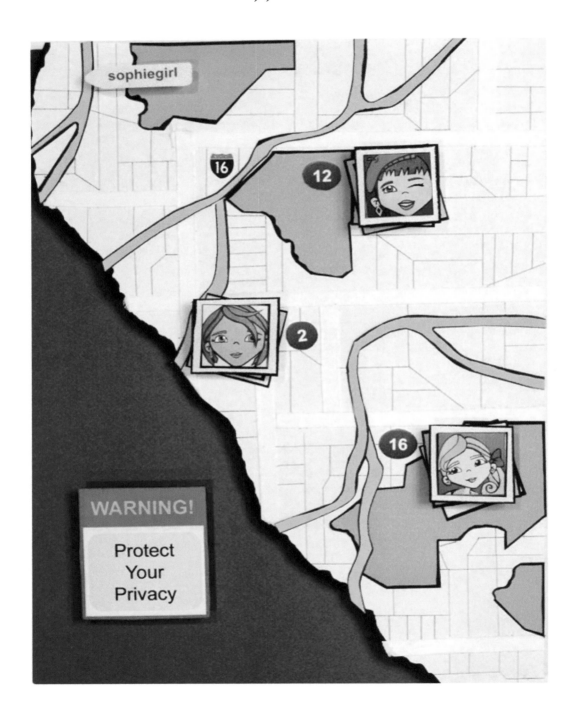

Protect Your Privacy

Private is NOT the default setting on most social media platforms. You wouldn't let a bunch of strangers into your house, so why in the world would you allow them to have access to so much personal information, like where you live and go to school? It is not necessary for you to include this information. If you don't already have a nickname, make one up. If you decide to use your name, make it your first name only. Because most smart phones encode the exact location of where pictures are taken, right down to the street address, I recommend you turn the geotagging feature OFF in your Settings. Do not share your passwords with friends or anyone else.

Beware of anyone you don't know 'in real life' trying to solicit personal information from you about your age, what state/town/city you live in, where you go to school, etc. Many child predators have become experts at disguising themselves as kids online and are easily able to make you feel as comfortable as if you were talking to one of your friends.

The internet is not your private diary. Your use of it should be thought of as a privilege and parents (who most likely pay your phone bill) should have access to your accounts in order to establish trust and to guide you as you learn your way around. Keep in mind that anything you do on your smart device (even if you've created a fake account in another name to avoid your cyberstalking parents) is tracked and linked directly to the registered name on the device you are using.

Work with a parent or other trusted adult to protect your privacy as much as possible online.

Drive

Congratulations, you can drive! Driving symbolizes freedom and independence, and with that comes responsibility. Now let's focus on the *road*, yes? And the brake lights in front of you, that guy's blind spot you're driving in, your mirrors, the stop sign or red light ahead, the pedestrian in the crosswalk—There are a million things to be watchful of when you are behind the wheel of that fabulous automobile. I wish there was a magic wand to be waved to make everyone, young people and grown-ups alike, understand how three or four seconds of distraction can change and potentially ruin your life or the life of someone else forever. If whatever it is can't wait, find a safe place to stop and use your phone.

Ask your Mom or Dad to tell you a story about how they survived in the pre-historic days before cell phones, before the phenomenon of being in constant contact with one another. You will never miss anything important enough to risk your own safety and the safety of those around you during the time it takes to get from point 'A' to point 'B'!

Etiquette

If you can't say something nice ... you know the rest, but to be clear: It is not ever, under any circumstance necessary to tell someone he or she is ugly.

Text-gossiping to your friend(s) across the room about the person sitting near you is immature and just plain rude.

Snooping through a friend's friend/follower/following lists for new friends is not cool.

Following or sending a request to an adult friend of your friend (i.e., her mom's best friend, her aunt, etc.) is not appropriate. With few exceptions, I do not believe adults should follow children who are not their own on social media sites.

Sharing, reposting or photos or artwork without permission or credit is rude and sometimes copyright infringement.

Tagging someone in a photo without their permission is thoughtless. If someone tags you in an unflattering photo or inappropriate post, you have every right to politely ask them to remove it. Check the social sites you use to see if you can choose a setting that either does not allow you to be tagged in posts or photos ever, or allows friends to tag you *with your approval* before it is added to your timeline.

Sharing photos from a party that you know a friend who wasn't invited will see is unnecessarily mean.

If two people are having an online conversation (e.g., on Facebook) that has nothing to do with you, don't interrupt.

If two people having a chat (that doesn't include you) in your feed or on your timeline, it is okay to politely ask that they take their conversation elsewhere.

When someone compliments you, simply say "thank you".

Social Stats

There are currently over 1.19 billion Facebook users around the world with over 665 million active users daily! Many people wrongly assume that "private" is the default setting on Facebook and other social sites. It isn't. The default setting is **Super Public**.

95% of **Facebook** users log into their accounts daily. Source: *Social Media Today*

There are more than 35 million #selfies posted to **Instagram**. Source: *MediaBistro*

There are 231.7 million monthly active **Twitter** users. Source: *Social Media Today*

Snapchat shares 400 million snaps per day, surpassing photo-sharing activity on both **Instagram** and **Facebook**. Source: *TechCrunch*

90% of teens using social-media who have witnessed online cruelty say they have ignored this behavior on social-media. Source: *PEW Research Center*

66% of teens who have witnessed online cruelty have also witnessed others joining in. Source: *PEW Research Center*

Ask Sophie

There's so much more to talk about. Let's continue the conversation!

Do you have a question about a tricky social situation? Ask Sophie and find other useful information at www.sophietakesaselfie.com.

You can also find us on Facebook, and on Instagram and Twitter @SophieSelfie.